The Ultimate Guide to Building Your ADU: From Concept to Completion

STEPH WYNNE

The Ultimate Guide to Building Your ADU: From Concept to Completion

Cover and interior images by Midjourney

For more information:

Skinny Books Publishing
20812 Ventura Blvd 200
Woodland Hills, CA 91364

www.skinnybookspublishing.com

ISBN: 9798333167897

Disclaimer

The information provided in this book is for educational and informational purposes only. It is not intended to be, nor should it be considered, legal or financial advice. Readers should consult with their own legal, accounting, and financial advisors before making any business decisions.

The case studies included are fictitious and are not based on real individuals or events.The characters and events portrayed in this book are fictitious people. Any similarity to real persons, living or dead, is coincidental and not intended by the author.

Table of Contents

Cheat Sheet: Overview of the process

Building an Accessory Dwelling Unit (ADU) in California involves several key steps and considerations.

Here is a overview of the process:

Research and Planning

Check Zoning and Regulations:

Eligibility: Ensure your property is eligible for an ADU. Most residentially zoned lots in Los Angeles can have an ADU, but specific requirements must be met.

Requirements: Familiarize yourself with local and state regulations, which have been streamlined to encourage ADU construction. Key requirements often include setback distances and maximum unit sizes.

Determine ADU Type:

Decide whether you want a detached, attached, garage conversion, basement conversion, or junior ADU.

Each type has different considerations and benefits depending on your property's layout and your needs.

Design and Permits

Hire Professionals:

Engage a Qualified Architect or Designer: This step is crucial to ensure your ADU design is functional and complies with all regulations. Design costs can range from $3,500 to $15,000 or more.

Submit Plans for Approval:

Permit Application: Submit your ADU plans to the Los Angeles Department of Building and Safety (LADBS) for approval.

California state laws require that ADU applications be approved or denied within 60 days. Permit fees can vary widely, typically ranging from $1,500 to $15,000 depending on the scope of your project.

Obtain Necessary Permits:

Ensure you obtain all relevant permits, including building, electrical, plumbing, and any other required permits to comply with local and state regulations.

Construction

Choosing a Contractor:

Select a Reputable Contractor: Choose a contractor with experience in building ADUs. Construction costs vary significantly based on the type and size of the ADU.

Garage conversions are generally the most cost-effective, ranging from $30,000 to $100,000, while new constructions can cost between $100,000 and $350,000 or more, depending on various factors.

Building Process:

Timeline: The construction process typically takes two to six months, depending on the project's complexity and whether you are converting existing space or building a new structure.

Compliance: Follow the approved plans and ensure compliance with all inspections and codes during construction.

Final Approvals and Occupancy

Inspections:

Compliance Checks: Throughout the construction process, various inspections will be required to ensure compliance with building codes and safety standards.

Certificate of Occupancy:

Final Approval: Once construction is complete and all inspections are passed, you will receive a Certificate of Occupancy.

This certificate allows you to legally rent out or use the ADU.

Additional Considerations:

Local Ordinances: Be aware of specific ordinances in Los

Angeles that may affect your ADU, such as additional requirements in Very High Fire Hazard Severity Zones and Hillside Areas.

Parking Requirements: Generally, no additional parking is required if the property is within ½ mile of public transit.

Permits: Ensure compliance with all local permit and approval requirements.

By following these steps and working with experienced professionals, you can successfully navigate the process of building an ADU in Los Angeles.

For more detailed information, you can visit the LADBS ADU guidelines and Los Angeles ADU Guide.

Chapter 1: What is an ADU?

An Accessory Dwelling Unit (ADU) is a secondary residential unit located on the same lot as a primary residence.

ADUs can either be attached to the main house or be completely detached structures.

These units are fully equipped with independent living facilities, including a kitchen, bathroom, and sleeping area.

Often referred to as granny flats, in-law units, backyard cottages, or secondary suites, ADUs provide flexible housing solutions for various needs, such as housing for family members, generating rental income, or serving as guest accommodations.

Key Features of ADUs

1. Independent Living Space: An ADU provides a self-contained living area that includes a kitchen, bathroom, and sleeping space.

This makes it a fully functional residential unit separate from the main house.

2. Attached or Detached: ADUs can be part of the main residence (attached) or a separate structure (detached) located on the same property.

This flexibility allows homeowners to choose the best option for their property and needs.

3. Compliance with Regulations: ADUs must comply with local and state regulations, which dictate aspects such as size, setbacks, height, and parking requirements. These regulations ensure that ADUs are safe, functional, and compatible with the neighborhood.

Case Study: Building a Detached ADU in Los Angeles

To illustrate the concept and benefits of ADUs, let's explore the experience of John and Mary, homeowners in Los Angeles who decided to build a detached ADU on their property.

Background:

John and Mary own a single-family home in a residential neighborhood of Los Angeles.

With their children grown and moved out, they wanted to utilize their spacious backyard to generate additional income and provide a living space for Mary's elderly mother.

After researching their options, they decided that building a detached ADU was the best solution.

Planning and Design:

They started by consulting with an architect experienced in ADU designs.

The architect helped them develop a plan for a 600-square-foot detached ADU that included a small kitchen, bathroom, living area, and a bedroom.

The design also featured a small patio area to provide outdoor space for Mary's mother.

Permitting Process:

John and Mary submitted their ADU plans to the Los Angeles Department of Building and Safety. The plans had to comply with local zoning regulations, which included:

Ensuring the ADU was at least 4 feet from the rear and side property lines.

Meeting the maximum size requirement of 1,200 square feet for detached ADUs.

Providing one additional parking space unless certain exemptions applied (e.g., being within ½ mile of public transit).

The permitting process involved several steps:

1. Plan Review: The city reviewed their plans for compliance with zoning and building codes.

2. Environmental Considerations: They ensured the ADU did not impact protected trees or wildlife.

3. Utilities: They planned for water, sewer, and electrical connections to the ADU.

Construction:

Once the permits were approved, John and Mary hired a licensed contractor to build the ADU.

Construction took about six months, during which they regularly communicated with the contractor to ensure the project stayed on track and within budget.

Outcome:

The completed ADU provided a comfortable and private living space for Mary's mother, allowing her to live independently while being close to family.

Additionally, the ADU significantly increased the property's value and provided the potential for rental income in the future.

Benefits Experienced:

1. Flexibility: The ADU offered a versatile living space that could be used for family, guests, or as a rental unit.
2. Increased Property Value: The ADU added value to their property, making it more attractive to future buyers.

3. Income Potential: The ADU provided a source of rental income, helping to offset the costs of the initial investment.

By exploring John and Mary's experience, we can see how ADUs offer practical solutions for homeowners looking to maximize their property's potential while providing flexible living arrangements for family members or tenants.

The process, while requiring careful planning and adherence to regulations, ultimately resulted in a valuable and multifunctional addition to their home.

Chapter 2: Types of ADUs

Accessory Dwelling Units (ADUs) offer a variety of configurations to suit different needs and property layouts.

Understanding the types of ADUs available helps homeowners make informed decisions.

This chapter provides detailed descriptions, examples, and the pros and cons of each ADU type, concluding with a case study to illustrate practical application.

1. Detached ADU

Description: A detached ADU is a standalone structure separate from the primary residence, typically located in the backyard.

Examples:

A small cottage or tiny house. Custom-built structures that complement the main house.

Pros:

- Greater privacy for both the primary residence and the ADU occupants.
- Flexibility in design and layout.
- Potential for higher rental income due to increased privacy.

Cons:

- Higher construction costs compared to attached ADUs.
- Requires more space on the property.
- May need separate utility connections.

Suitable Applications:

- Housing for elderly parents or adult children.
- Rental income.
- Home office or studio space.

2. Attached ADU

Description: An attached ADU is an additional unit built as an extension to the main house, sharing at least one wall with the primary residence.

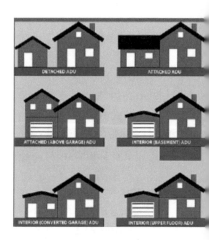

Examples:

- An extension with a separate entrance.
- A converted attached garage.

Pros:

- Lower construction costs than detached ADUs.
- Easier access to existing utilities.
- Utilizes existing structures.

Cons:

- Less privacy than detached ADUs.
- Design may be constrained by the existing structure.

Suitable Applications:

- Close supervision of elderly family members.
- Moderate privacy rental unit.
- Expanding living space with minimal structural changes.

3. Garage Conversion

Description: A garage conversion involves transforming an existing garage into a livable ADU, making use of the existing structure.

Examples:

- A single-car garage turned into a studio apartment.
- A two-car garage converted into a one-bedroom ADU.

Pros:

- Lower construction costs due to existing structure.
- Minimal impact on property's exterior.
- Quick conversion process.

Cons:

- Limited space depending on garage size.
- Potential zoning and permit challenges.
- Reduces parking space for the main house.

Suitable Applications:

- Affordable rental units.
- Guest accommodations.
- Home office or workspace.

4. Basement Conversion

Description: A basement conversion involves remodeling an existing basement into a self-contained living unit.

Examples:

- A full basement transformed into a one-bedroom apartment.
- Partial basement conversion with kitchenette and bathroom.

Pros:

- Utilizes existing space, reducing construction costs.
- Maintains property's exterior appearance.
- Provides a cool and insulated living space.

Cons:

- Potential moisture and ventilation issues.
- Limited natural light.
- May require extensive remodeling to meet building codes.

Suitable Applications:

- Rental unit for additional income.
- Living space for family members.
- Home gym or recreational area.

5. Junior ADU (JADU)

Description: A Junior ADU (JADU) is a smaller unit (up to 500 square feet) created within the walls of an existing single-family home, often sharing some facilities with the main house.

Examples:

- A converted bedroom with an efficient kitchen.
- A section of the house with a separate entrance and shared bathroom.

Pros:

- Low construction costs.
- Easy access to existing utilities.
- Minimal impact on property layout.

Cons:

- Limited space.
- Shared facilities may reduce privacy.
- Zoning restrictions may apply.

Suitable Applications:

- Housing for a single tenant or caregiver.
- Short-term rental space.
- Home office or studio.

Case Study: Garage Conversion in San Diego

Background:

Sarah and Mike, a couple in San Diego, decided to convert their two-car garage into a one-bedroom ADU to generate rental income.

They wanted an affordable solution that would not significantly alter their property's appearance.

Planning and Design:

They hired an architect to design a functional layout that included a small kitchen, bathroom, and living area within the garage space.

The design also featured large windows to maximize natural light.

Permitting Process:

Sarah and Mike submitted their plans to the San Diego Planning Department. The main considerations included:

- Ensuring the ADU met the size requirements.
- Addressing any zoning and setback regulations.
- Obtaining necessary permits for electrical, plumbing, and structural changes.

Construction:

The conversion process took about three months. The couple worked with a licensed contractor who handled the remodeling, including:

- Installing insulation and drywall.
- Adding plumbing and electrical systems.
- Finishing with flooring, paint, and fixtures.

Outcome:

The garage conversion resulted in a cozy one-bedroom ADU that was quickly rented out to a young professional.

The rental income significantly helped Sarah and Mike with their mortgage payments.

Benefits Experienced:

Affordable Construction: Utilizing the existing garage structure kept costs low.

Quick Turnaround: The project was completed in a relatively short time frame.

Increased Property Value: The ADU added value to their home and provided a steady rental income.

By exploring Sarah and Mike's experience, we can see how a garage conversion ADU offers a cost-effective and efficient solution for homeowners looking to maximize their property's potential while providing a valuable living space.

Each type of ADU has its unique benefits and considerations, making it essential for homeowners to choose the one that best fits their needs and property layout.

Chapter 3: What's the ADU Process?

Building an Accessory Dwelling Unit (ADU) involves several steps from initial planning to final approvals.

This chapter provides a detailed, step-by-step guide to help homeowners navigate the entire process, along with checklists and timelines to stay organized.

A case study at the end illustrates the practical application of these steps.

Step-by-Step Guide to Building an ADU

1. Initial Research and Planning

Check Zoning and Regulations: Verify your property's eligibility for an ADU by checking local zoning laws and regulations.

Contact your city's planning department or check their website for specific requirements.

Checklist:

- ☐ Verify zoning eligibility
- ☐ Review local ADU ordinances
- ☐ Identify any restrictions or requirements

Determine ADU Type: Decide whether you want a detached, attached, garage conversion, or basement conversion ADU.

Consider the space available, your budget, and your intended use for the ADU.

Checklist:

- ☐ Evaluate property layout
- ☐ Choose ADU type (detached, attached, conversion)

2. Design and Permits

Hire Professionals: Engage an architect or designer to create detailed plans that comply with local regulations.

This is crucial for ensuring the ADU meets all safety and building standards.

Checklist:

- ☐ Hire an architect or designer
- ☐ Develop ADU plans

Submit Plans for Approval: Submit your ADU plans to the local planning department for review.

This includes zoning review, building permits, and any other necessary approvals.

Checklist:

- ☐ Submit plans to planning department
- ☐ Obtain zoning approval
- ☐ Secure building permits

Utility Planning: Plan for utility connections such as water, sewer, electricity, and gas.

Ensure these are included in your design plans and comply with local requirements.

Checklist:

- [ ] Plan utility connections
- [ ] Include utilities in design plans

3. Construction

Hire a Contractor: Choose a licensed contractor experienced in ADU construction. Get multiple quotes and check references to ensure quality and reliability.

Checklist:

- [ ] Select a licensed contractor
- [ ] Obtain construction quotes
- [ ] Check contractor references

Begin Construction: With permits in hand, start the construction process. Regularly communicate with your contractor to ensure the project stays on track and within budget.

Checklist:

- [ ] Start construction
- [ ] Monitor progress
- [ ] Maintain communication with contractor

4. Inspections and Final Approvals

Conduct Inspections: During construction, various inspections will be required to ensure the ADU meets all building codes and safety standards.

Schedule inspections at key stages, such as foundation, framing, and final inspection.

Checklist:

- ☐ Schedule necessary inspections
- ☐ Pass all building inspections

Obtain Certificate of Occupancy: Once construction and inspections are complete, apply for a Certificate of Occupancy.

This document confirms the ADU is safe and ready for use.

Checklist:

- ☐ Apply for Certificate of Occupancy
- ☐ Receive final approval
- ☐ Timelines

Research and Planning: 1-2 months

- ☐ Design and Permits: 2-4 months
- ☐ Construction: 3-6 months
- ☐ Inspections and Final Approvals: 1-2 months

Case Study: Building a Detached ADU in Los Angeles

Background:

David and Lisa, a couple in Los Angeles, decided to build a detached ADU in their backyard to generate rental income and provide a living space for Lisa's mother.

Initial Research and Planning:

David and Lisa started by checking the local zoning laws and found that their property was eligible for a detached ADU. They decided on a detached ADU because it provided the most privacy for Lisa's mother.

Design and Permits:

They hired an architect to design a 600-square-foot ADU with a kitchen, bathroom, living area, and bedroom. The design included energy-efficient features and large windows for natural light.

They submitted their plans to the Los Angeles Department of Building and Safety and received approval within three months.

Construction:

David and Lisa hired a licensed contractor to begin construction.

The process took about five months, during which they communicated regularly with the contractor to ensure the project stayed on track.

They encountered a minor setback when an unexpected plumbing issue arose, but it was resolved quickly with the help of their contractor.

Inspections and Final Approvals:

Throughout the construction, the ADU underwent several inspections to ensure compliance with building codes. After passing all inspections, David and Lisa applied for and received the Certificate of Occupancy, allowing them to legally rent out the ADU.

Outcome:

The ADU provided a comfortable and private living space for Lisa's mother, and when she later moved, it became a rental unit that generated steady income for David and Lisa.

Benefits Experienced:

Additional Income: The rental income helped offset their mortgage payments.

Increased Property Value: The ADU added significant value to their property.

Flexible Use: The ADU served both as a family living space and a rental unit.

By following the step-by-step process and staying organized with checklists and timelines, David and Lisa successfully built their ADU, illustrating the practical application and benefits of ADU development.

Chapter 4: Pros and Cons of Building or Buying a Pre-Built ADU

As homeowners consider adding an Accessory Dwelling Unit (ADU) to their property, they face the decision of whether to build a custom ADU or purchase a pre-built unit.

Each option has its unique advantages and disadvantages, and the choice depends on individual needs, circumstances, and budget.

This chapter analyzes the pros and cons of both options and provides a case study to illustrate the potential pitfalls of not obtaining the necessary permits.

Building a Custom ADU

Pros:

1. Customization: Homeowners can design the ADU to their specific needs and preferences, ensuring that the unit complements the main house and maximizes the available space.

2. Quality Control: By overseeing the construction process, homeowners can ensure that high-quality materials and construction practices are used.

3. Integration: Custom ADUs can be better integrated into the existing landscape and architecture of the property, maintaining aesthetic consistency.

Cons:

1. Higher Costs: Custom ADUs typically have higher upfront costs due to design fees, permits, and construction expenses.

2. Longer Timeline: The process of designing, obtaining permits, and constructing a custom ADU can take several months or even years.

3. Project Management: Managing a construction project requires time, effort, and expertise, which can be challenging for homeowners.

Buying a Pre-Built ADU

Pros:

1. Lower Costs: Pre-built ADUs are generally more affordable as they benefit from mass production and economies of scale.

2. Faster Installation: Pre-built units can be installed quickly, often within a few days to a few weeks, significantly reducing the time to occupancy.

3. Minimal Disruption: The construction and assembly of pre-built units occur off-site, minimizing disruption to the homeowner's daily life and property.

Cons:

1. Limited Customization: Pre-built ADUs offer limited design options, which may not fully meet the homeowner's needs or preferences.

2. Quality Variability: The quality of pre-built units can vary, and homeowners may have less control over construction materials and methods.

3. Integration Challenges: Pre-built ADUs may not blend seamlessly with the existing property, potentially affecting the overall aesthetic and functionality.

Case Study: Flipping Houses Without Proper Permits

Background:

John, a single man who flips houses for a living, decided to add a pre-built ADU to one of his properties in Los Angeles to increase its value and appeal to potential buyers.

He found a great deal on a pre-built unit and had it installed quickly to stay on schedule for his next flip.

The Mistake:

Eager to complete the project, John did not obtain the necessary city permits for the ADU installation. He assumed that since the unit was pre-built, it wouldn't require the same rigorous permitting process as a custom-built ADU.

The Consequences:

Code Violations: During a routine inspection, the city discovered the unpermitted ADU. John was cited for multiple code violations, including improper utility hookups and non-compliance with setback requirements.

Fines and Penalties: John faced substantial fines for the violations and was required to halt all work on the property until the issues were resolved.

Additional Costs: To bring the ADU into compliance, John had to hire a contractor to make necessary modifications, obtain retroactive permits, and pay all associated fees. This added significant unplanned expenses to his project.

Project Delays: The permitting and compliance process took several months, delaying the sale of the property and reducing his potential profits.

The Outcome:

Ultimately, John learned a valuable lesson about the importance of obtaining proper permits, even for pre-built ADUs.

The additional costs and delays severely impacted his bottom line, and he became more diligent in ensuring all future projects complied with local regulations.

Lessons Learned:

1. Always Obtain Permits: Regardless of whether the ADU is custom-built or pre-built, securing the necessary permits is crucial to avoid legal and financial repercussions.

2. Do Your Research: Understand local zoning laws, building codes, and permit requirements before starting any construction project.

3. Plan for Contingencies: Include a buffer in your budget and timeline to account for unexpected issues that may arise during the permitting and construction process.

Conclusion

Deciding between building a custom ADU or buying a pre-built unit depends on various factors, including budget, timeline, and personal preferences.

Both options have their pros and cons, and homeowners must carefully consider these aspects to make an informed decision.

Additionally, adhering to local regulations and obtaining the necessary permits is essential to avoid costly mistakes and ensure the successful completion of the project.

By learning from the experiences of others, such as John's case, homeowners can navigate the ADU process more effectively and achieve their goals.

Chapter 5: How ADUs Work and Why They're Important

Accessory Dwelling Units (ADUs) are an increasingly popular solution for addressing housing shortages, providing affordable rental options, and offering flexible living arrangements.

This chapter explores the functionality of ADUs and their significance in modern housing landscapes. A case study illustrates the real-world impact of ADUs.

The Functionality of ADUs

1. Independent Living Spaces:

ADUs provide complete, self-contained living units with their own kitchen, bathroom, and sleeping areas.

This independence makes them suitable for various uses, such as housing family members, generating rental income, or serving as guest accommodations.

2. Versatile Housing Solutions:

ADUs can be customized to fit different needs and property layouts. They can be detached units, attached extensions, garage conversions, or basement apartments.

This versatility allows homeowners to choose the best option for their specific circumstances.

3. Affordable Housing:

ADUs offer a cost-effective housing solution compared to building new single-family homes or apartment complexes. They utilize existing land and infrastructure, reducing overall construction costs. This affordability makes ADUs an attractive option for renters seeking lower-cost housing.

The Importance of ADUs

1. Addressing Housing Shortages:

In many urban areas, housing shortages have driven up rental prices and made it difficult for people to find affordable homes.

ADUs increase the housing supply by adding new units to existing residential lots, helping to alleviate these shortages

2. Providing Affordable Rental Options:

ADUs offer more affordable rental options compared to traditional apartments. They provide a practical solution for renters who need lower-cost housing but want to live in established neighborhoods with access to amenities and services.

3. Offering Flexible Living Solutions:

ADUs provide flexibility for homeowners and renters alike. They can be used to house elderly family members, provide living space for adult children, or serve as rental units for additional income.

This flexibility helps families adapt to changing needs over time.

4. Promoting Sustainable Living:

By making use of existing land and resources, ADUs promote sustainable living practices. They help reduce urban expansion, minimize environmental impact, and make efficient use of available space in residential areas.

Case Study: Creating an Affordable Rental ADU in San Francisco

Background:

Mark, a homeowner in San Francisco, decided to convert his unused basement into an ADU to provide affordable housing for a local teacher.

With the high cost of living in the city, Mark wanted to make a meaningful contribution to the community while also generating some rental income.

Planning and Design:

Mark hired an architect to design a functional one-bedroom apartment in his basement. The design included a small kitchen, bathroom, living area, and bedroom.

Mark prioritized energy-efficient features and used sustainable materials to minimize the environmental impact.

Permitting Process:

Mark submitted his plans to the San Francisco Planning Department. The main considerations included:

- Ensuring compliance with local zoning regulations.
- Addressing any required setbacks and utility connections.
- Obtaining necessary permits for electrical, plumbing, and structural modifications.

Construction:

The construction process took about four months. Mark worked with a licensed contractor who handled the remodeling, including:

- Installing insulation and drywall.
- Adding plumbing and electrical systems.
- Finishing with flooring, paint, and fixtures.

Outcome:

The basement conversion resulted in a comfortable and affordable one-bedroom apartment. Mark rented the ADU to a local teacher, providing much-needed affordable housing in a high-cost city. The rental income also helped Mark cover his mortgage and property taxes.

Benefits Experienced:

Affordable Housing: The ADU provided an affordable rental option in a city with high living costs.

Community Contribution: Mark's ADU helped address the local housing shortage and supported a community member.

Additional Income: The rental income supplemented Mark's finances, easing his financial burden.

Conclusion

ADUs play a crucial role in addressing housing shortages, offering affordable rental options, and providing flexible living solutions. By creating independent living spaces on existing residential properties, ADUs maximize the use of available land and resources.

As demonstrated by Mark's experience, ADUs can have a positive impact on both homeowners and the community, making them a valuable component of modern housing strategies.

Chapter 6: Frequently Asked Questions about ADUs

Can I build an ADU in California?

Yes, homeowners in California can build ADUs under new laws. Existing buildings can also be converted into ADUs.

Where are ADUs allowed?

ADUs are allowed in all residential zones with limited exceptions for public safety, traffic, and water. Homeowners Associations cannot ban ADUs.

Are there parking requirements for ADUs?

Under new laws, there are fewer or no parking requirements for ADUs.

Can unpermitted ADUs be legalized?

State law now allows homeowners to bring ADUs built without permits into compliance, using building standards from when the ADUs were constructed and offering a five-year amnesty period.

What spaces can be converted into ADUs?

Many existing spaces, like garages, parts of the main house, attics, and basements, can be converted into ADUs. Single-family zones are required.

Is owner occupancy required?

For ADUs built between 2020 and 2025, owner occupancy rules have been banned. However, this requirement still applies to Junior ADUs (JADUs).

What can I build?

Floor Area Ratios (FARs): *Each city has different methods to calculate floor area.*

Lot Size: *Cities can no longer consider lot size when approving ADUs.*

How will building an ADU affect my taxes?

Property taxes will increase as the ADU adds value. ADU rent is taxable, but maintenance and construction costs can be deducted. You might also have to pay capital gains tax when you sell your property.

What fees can I expect?

Fees vary by city and project. Typically, fees range around $10,000, or less than 5% of the construction cost. These fees must be paid before getting your building permit and can include:

- *Entitlement fees*
- *Building permit fees*
- *Development impact fees*
- *Local agency and special district fees*
- *School district impact fees*
- *Water and sewer connection fees*

Is an ADU a good investment?

Yes! The primary reason homeowners invest in ADUs is to generate additional income and increase property value.

Am I allowed to build an ADU?

In most cases, yes. You can build an ADU up to 800 sq ft, and many homeowners can build larger ADUs if they meet local city rules. Any legally built structure, like a garage or barn, can be converted into an ADU.

What are the building costs?

- ***Interior Conversion:*** *$20,000 to $50,000*
- ***High-End Unit:*** *$500,000 or more*
- ***Average Project:*** *$400 per square foot*
- ***Cost Variations:*** *Based on the type of ADU and design specifics*

Traditional ADU vs. Prefabricated ADU

- ***Traditional Construction:*** *Built on-site, flexible design*

- ***Prefabricated Construction:*** *Built off-site, quicker assembly, but consider transportation and installation costs*

Is there financial aid for ADUs?

Yes. The California Housing Finance Agency (CalHFA) offers ADU grants reimbursing qualifying homeowners for pre-development costs up to $40,000. The budget for 2024 has not been finalized.

Can I have multiple detached homes on one lot?

Yes, you can build one ADU on a lot with several detached single-family homes.

Are there size limits for ADUs?

Yes. The maximum size for attached ADUs can be a percentage of the primary dwelling. ADUs can exceed 1,200 square feet if local ordinances allow it.

How many ADUs are allowed on a multifamily site?

Up to two detached ADUs.

Can existing accessory structures be converted to ADUs?

Yes, existing structures like garages, sheds, and barns can be converted to ADUs.

What about rental terms?

Local agencies may require that the property be rented for more than 30 days.

How soon can I get approval to build?

If your property already has a single-family or multifamily dwelling, usually within 60 days of your application.

Does an ADU need its own address?

No, it's okay to have an ADU at the existing address, but you can request a separate fractional address if needed.

Does an ADU need its own utility meter?

No, but you can request a separate utility meter if desired.

Is there a need to separate the ADU from the main house?

Common walls must meet a sound transmission rating of STC 50 or higher. Google it!

When converting a garage into an ADU, what are typical issues?

Ceiling joists may need upgrading, and energy calculations are required for the new conditioned space.

Can I convert an unpermitted garage to an ADU?

You'll need a new building permit if there's no record of a garage permit. An ADU conversion would require an alteration permit.

Is there a distance requirement between an ADU and other structures?

Yes, building codes must be followed, and local agencies can impose development standards.

Is there a limit to how big an ADU can be regarding water sprinklers?

The Los Angeles County Fire Department requires an automatic sprinkler system in ADUs with a maximum living area of 1,200 square feet.

Can I use one heating unit for both the main house and the attached ADU?

No, each dwelling unit must have its own heating facilities.

Does the ADU sewer need a separate connection?

Yes, buildings with ADUs must have their own sewers, according to the plumbing code.

Do local agencies have to adopt ADU ordinances?

No, but if they do, they must submit a copy to the Housing Community Development (HCD) within 60 days.

Are ADUs subject to setbacks?

Yes, local agencies can impose setbacks for ADUs.

Is the California Coastal Zone affected by new ADU laws?

Yes, but the laws do not change the Coastal Act's impact on jurisdictions within the zone.

Does Senate Bill (SB) 9 impact ADUs?

Yes, SB 9 overlaps with State ADU Law on some topics.

Frequently Asked Pre-Built ADU Questions

Pre-built ADUs like Boxabl are gaining popularity. Boxabl ADUs are weather-resistant, quick to set up, and come ready to plug into site utilities.

They cost around $60,000 plus shipping, but this doesn't include land, site setup, utility hookups, or foundation.

Is the Boxabl VA loan friendly?

They are expected to be compatible with most existing loan mortgage programs.

What utilities and solar options are available?

Boxabl ADUs can connect to standard utilities, water tanks, and solar panels.

Are they durable in extreme weather?

Yes, Boxabl ADUs are tested for hurricanes, earthquakes, and other extreme conditions.

For more information, visit [Boxabl](https://www.boxabl.com) or email hello@boxabl.com.

Chapter 7: Summary of New ADU Laws

Recent changes in Accessory Dwelling Unit (ADU) laws at the state and local levels have significantly impacted homeowners, making it easier to build and legalize ADUs.

These changes aim to address the housing crisis, promote affordable housing, and streamline the ADU construction process.

This chapter provides an overview of these new laws and their implications for homeowners.

State-Level Changes

1. Streamlined Permitting Process

AB 68 and AB 881: These bills require local agencies to approve or deny ADU permit applications within 60 days, a reduction from the previous 120-day period.

They also prohibit the application of development standards that limit the construction of at least one ADU and one Junior ADU (JADU) per residential lot, regardless of lot size.

Implications: Homeowners can expect faster permit approvals, reducing delays in construction projects.

2. Expanded Allowable ADU Sizes and Types

SB 13: This law allows ADUs up to 1,200 square feet and eliminates the requirement for additional parking spaces if the ADU is within half a mile of public transit. It also removes the owner-occupancy requirement until 2025.

Implications: Homeowners have more flexibility in designing larger ADUs and face fewer parking-related restrictions.

3. Amnesty for Unpermitted ADUs

AB 670 and AB 671: These laws create pathways for unpermitted ADUs to be legalized, including a five-year amnesty period during which homeowners can bring their ADUs up to code without facing penalties.

Implications: Homeowners with existing unpermitted ADUs can legalize their units, increasing the availability of affordable housing.

Local-Level Changes

1. Local Ordinances and Development Standards

Many cities and counties have updated their local ordinances to comply with state laws, often adding specific development standards tailored to their communities.

These may include additional setback requirements, height restrictions, and design guidelines.

Example: Los Angeles has specific guidelines for ADUs in Very High Fire Hazard Severity Zones and Hillside Areas, including additional safety measures and restrictions.

Implications: Homeowners must review their local ordinances to ensure compliance with both state and local regulations.

2. Parking Requirements

While state laws have reduced parking requirements for ADUs, some localities have further relaxed these rules, especially in areas well-served by public transit.

Implications: Reduced parking requirements can lower the cost and complexity of building an ADU, particularly in urban areas.

3. Utility Connection Fees

Many local governments have adjusted utility connection fees to make them more affordable for ADU construction. Some areas offer fee waivers or reductions for smaller ADUs or those built for low-income tenants.

Implications: Lower utility connection fees can make ADU projects more financially viable for homeowners.

Chapter 8: Case Studies and Success Stories

Case Study 1: Garage Conversion in Los Angeles

Background:

Laura, a homeowner in Los Angeles, decided to convert her detached two-car garage into an ADU to generate rental income. She wanted to create a stylish, comfortable living space that would attract long-term tenants.

Planning and Design:

Laura hired an architect to design a modern studio apartment with a full kitchen and bathroom. The design included large windows to bring in natural light and an open floor plan to maximize the limited space.

Permitting Process:

Laura faced challenges with zoning regulations and setback requirements. However, by working closely with the Los Angeles Department of Building and Safety and her architect, she was able to adjust the plans to meet all local codes.

Construction:

The construction took four months. Laura chose eco-friendly materials and energy-efficient appliances, which increased upfront costs but would save money in the long run.

Outcome:

The ADU was completed on time and within budget. Laura quickly found a tenant, a young professional who appreciated the modern amenities and location.

Benefits Experienced:

Rental Income: The ADU provided a steady stream of rental income, helping Laura offset her mortgage payments.

Property Value: The ADU increased the overall value of Laura's property.

Sustainability: Using eco-friendly materials and appliances reduced utility costs and had a positive environmental impact.

Lessons Learned:

Flexibility in Design: Being open to design adjustments helped Laura navigate zoning regulations and achieve her goals.

Importance of Professional Help: Hiring an experienced architect and contractor was crucial in overcoming regulatory hurdles and ensuring high-quality construction.

Case Study 2: Basement Conversion in San Francisco

Background:

Robert, a homeowner in San Francisco, wanted to convert his unused basement into an ADU to provide affordable housing for his elderly parents.

He needed the space to be accessible and comfortable while adhering to local building codes.

Planning and Design:

Robert collaborated with a design firm specializing in accessible living spaces. The design included a bedroom, bathroom, kitchenette, and living area, all on one level with no steps.

Features like grab bars, wide doorways, and non-slip flooring were incorporated for safety.

Permitting Process:

The San Francisco Planning Department required detailed plans to ensure compliance with accessibility standards and building codes.

The permitting process took longer than expected due to additional requirements for accessibility modifications.

Construction:

Construction took about five months. Robert worked with a contractor experienced in accessibility adaptations. The contractor installed insulation, updated plumbing and electrical systems, and finished the space with high-quality, durable materials.

Outcome:

The basement ADU provided a safe, comfortable living space for Robert's parents. The accessibility features made daily living easier for them, and they were happy to be close to family.

Benefits Experienced:

Family Proximity: The ADU allowed Robert's parents to live independently while staying close to family.

Increased Home Value: The accessibility features and high-quality finishes increased the home's market value.

Cost Savings: The ADU saved on costs compared to moving Robert's parents into an assisted living facility.

Lessons Learned:

Planning for Accessibility: Incorporating accessibility features requires careful planning and adherence to additional regulations.

Patience with Permits: The permitting process for accessibility modifications can be lengthy, so patience and thorough documentation are essential.

Case Study 3: Detached ADU in Reseda

Background:

Samantha, a homeowner in Reseda, wanted to build a detached ADU in her backyard to create a flexible living space for her family.

Her goal was to use the ADU as a guest house, rental unit, and potentially a home office.

Planning and Design:

Samantha worked with an architect to design a 700-square-foot ADU with a loft bedroom, full kitchen, bathroom, and living area. The design emphasized open spaces, natural light, and modern aesthetics.

Permitting Process:

Reseda's permitting process for ADUs is streamlined, but Samantha still needed to ensure compliance with setback, height, and design regulations.

She faced minor delays due to neighborhood reviews and had to adjust her plans slightly to meet all requirements.

Construction:

Construction took about six months. Samantha chose a contractor with experience in building ADUs. The project included site preparation, foundation work, framing, and finishing touches like landscaping and exterior lighting.

Outcome:

The ADU was completed successfully and served multiple purposes over time.

Initially, it housed a relative who needed temporary accommodation.

Later, Samantha rented it out to generate income and eventually used it as a home office during the COVID-19 pandemic.

Benefits Experienced:

Versatility: The ADU provided flexible space that adapted to Samantha's changing needs over time.

Rental Income: When rented, the ADU generated additional income, helping cover household expenses.

Enhanced Lifestyle: The ADU offered a private, quiet space for working from home, improving Samantha's work-life balance.

Lessons Learned:

Future-Proof Design: Designing the ADU with flexibility in mind allowed Samantha to adapt its use over time.

Community Engagement: Addressing neighborhood concerns and involving the community early in the process helped smooth the permitting process.

Quality Construction: Investing in quality materials and a reputable contractor ensured the ADU's durability and long-term value.

Conclusion

These case studies demonstrate the diverse applications and benefits of ADUs, from generating rental income and providing affordable housing to offering flexible living solutions.

Homeowners can learn from these examples to navigate the challenges and maximize the potential of their own ADU projects.

Each project highlights the importance of planning, professional help, and adherence to regulations to achieve successful outcomes.

Chapter 9: Design Considerations for ADUs

Designing an Accessory Dwelling Unit (ADU) requires careful consideration of various factors to ensure the space is functional, aesthetically pleasing, sustainable, and accessible.

This chapter offers tips and best practices for optimizing space, integrating with existing structures, promoting sustainability, and enhancing accessibility.

A case study illustrates the importance of balancing design aspirations with budget constraints.

Space Optimization

1. Utilize Vertical Space

- Incorporate lofts or mezzanines for sleeping areas or storage to maximize floor space.

- Use tall shelving and cabinetry to make use of vertical space for storage.

2. Multi-Functional Furniture

- Invest in furniture that serves multiple purposes, such as sofa beds, fold-out tables, and storage ottomans.

3. Open Floor Plans

- Open floor plans can make small spaces feel larger and more flexible.

- Use sliding doors or room dividers to create privacy without compromising on space.

4. Built-In Storage

Integrate built-in storage solutions like under-stair storage, built-in benches with storage, and recessed shelves to save space.

Aesthetic Integration

1. Harmonize with the Main House

- Match the architectural style, materials, and colors of the ADU with the primary residence for visual cohesion.
- Use similar landscaping elements to create a seamless transition between the ADU and the main house.

2. High-Quality Finishes

- Invest in durable and high-quality finishes that enhance the aesthetic appeal and longevity of the ADU.

3. Natural Light

- Maximize natural light with large windows, skylights, and glass doors to create a bright and inviting space.
- Use light-colored walls and reflective surfaces to amplify natural light.

Sustainability

1. Energy Efficiency

- Incorporate energy-efficient appliances, LED lighting, and programmable thermostats to reduce energy consumption.

- Use high-performance insulation and windows to improve thermal performance.

2. Sustainable Materials

- Choose sustainable building materials like reclaimed wood, bamboo, and recycled steel.
- Opt for non-toxic paints and finishes to improve indoor air quality.

3. Water Conservation

- Install low-flow fixtures and water-efficient appliances to conserve water.
- Consider rainwater harvesting systems for irrigation.

Accessibility

1. Universal Design Principles

- Design the ADU with universal design principles to accommodate people of all ages and abilities.
- Include features like wide doorways, zero-step entries, and lever-style door handles.

2. Adaptable Layouts

- Plan for adaptable layouts that can be easily modified to meet changing needs, such as adding grab bars or lowering countertops.

3. Safety Features

Install non-slip flooring, good lighting, and easily accessible emergency exits to enhance safety.

Case Study: Balancing Design Aspirations with Budget Constraints

Background:

Sarah and James, a couple from Sacramento, decided to build an ADU in their backyard. Sarah wanted a complex design featuring high-end finishes, a loft area, and sustainable materials.

James, aware of their limited budget, knew they needed to make practical decisions to stay within their financial means.

Planning and Design:

Sarah envisioned a 600-square-foot ADU with a modern loft, high ceilings, large windows, and luxurious finishes. She also wanted eco-friendly materials and energy-efficient systems.

James, on the other hand, was concerned about the costs and wanted to ensure the project was financially viable.

Compromise and Collaboration:

The couple worked with an architect to find a balance between Sarah's design aspirations and James's budget concerns. They made the following compromises:

Loft Area: They included a loft for the sleeping area to save floor space but opted for a simpler design without custom stairs.

Windows and Light: They maximized natural light with strategically placed large windows but chose standard sizes to reduce costs.

Materials: They selected mid-range sustainable materials instead of high-end options, ensuring eco-friendliness without overspending.

Finishes: They opted for high-quality but affordable finishes, focusing on areas that added the most value and visual impact.

Construction:

The construction took about seven months. The contractor adhered to the budget by sourcing materials locally and using efficient construction techniques.

Regular meetings with the architect and contractor helped keep the project on track and within budget.

Outcome:

The ADU was completed successfully, meeting both Sarah's design goals and James's budget constraints.

The space was bright, modern, and sustainable, offering a functional living area that could be rented out or used for guests.

Benefits Experienced:

Financial Viability: By compromising on certain aspects, they kept the project within budget.

Aesthetic Appeal: The ADU was visually appealing and harmonized well with their main house.

Sustainability: They achieved an eco-friendly design using mid-range sustainable materials.

Lessons Learned:

Effective Communication: Clear communication and compromise between Sarah and James ensured that both design aspirations and budget constraints were met.

Professional Guidance: Working with an architect and contractor helped them make informed decisions and stay on budget.

Prioritization: Focusing on essential features and being flexible with other aspects allowed them to achieve a beautiful and functional ADU without overspending.

Conclusion

Designing an ADU requires careful consideration of space optimization, aesthetic integration, sustainability, and accessibility.

By balancing design aspirations with practical constraints, homeowners can create functional and attractive ADUs that meet their needs and budget.

Learning from real-life experiences, like Sarah and James's project, highlights the importance of collaboration, professional guidance, and prioritization in achieving successful outcomes.

Chapter 10: Financing Your ADU Project

Financing an Accessory Dwelling Unit (ADU) can be a complex process, but understanding the various options available can help homeowners find the best solution for their needs.

This chapter explores different financing methods, including home equity loans, construction loans, government grants, and private financing. It also provides guidance on selecting the most suitable funding source.

A case study at the end demonstrates how to build a cost-effective ADU on a tight budget.

Financing Options

1. Home Equity Loans

Description: Home equity loans allow homeowners to borrow against the equity in their home. These loans typically have fixed interest rates and are repaid over a set period.

Pros:

- Fixed interest rates provide predictable payments.
- Interest may be tax-deductible.
- Can fund the entire ADU project.

Cons:

- Requires sufficient home equity.
- Puts your home at risk if you fail to make payments.

Best For: Homeowners with substantial equity who prefer fixed monthly payments.

2. Home Equity Line of Credit (HELOC)

Description: A HELOC is a revolving line of credit secured by your home's equity. It functions like a credit card, allowing you to borrow up to a certain limit and repay as needed.

Pros:

- Flexible borrowing and repayment terms.
- Interest is only paid on the amount borrowed.
- Typically lower interest rates than personal loans or credit cards.

Cons:

- Variable interest rates can lead to fluctuating payments.
- Requires sufficient home equity.
- Risk of foreclosure if payments are not made.

Best For: Homeowners who need flexible access to funds over time.

3. Construction Loans

Description: Construction loans are short-term loans specifically designed to finance the building of a new home or major renovations. They are typically converted to a mortgage once the construction is complete.

Pros:

- Funds are released in stages as construction progresses.
- Interest is only paid on the amount disbursed.
- Converts to a mortgage, simplifying repayment.

Cons:

- Requires detailed construction plans and cost estimates.
- Higher interest rates than traditional mortgages.
- Short-term duration can be challenging for complex projects.

Best For: Homeowners undertaking substantial construction projects who need funds disbursed in stages.

4. Government Grants and Incentives

Description: Various federal, state, and local government programs offer grants and incentives to encourage the construction of ADUs.

These can include tax credits, low-interest loans, and direct grants.

Pros:

- Reduces overall project cost.
- Encourages sustainable and affordable housing development.
- May not require repayment.

Cons:

- Competitive application process.
- May have specific eligibility requirements and restrictions.
- Limited funding amounts.

Best For: Homeowners who qualify for specific grants and are willing to navigate the application process.

5. Private Financing

Description: Private financing includes personal loans, financing through ADU builders, and crowdfunding. Personal loans are unsecured loans with fixed interest rates, while some ADU builders offer financing plans.

Pros:

- Quick access to funds.
- Flexible terms and conditions.
- Can be an option for those with limited home equity.

Cons:

- Higher interest rates compared to secured loans.
- Shorter repayment terms can lead to higher monthly payments.
- Personal loans may have lower borrowing limits.

Best For: Homeowners with limited home equity or those seeking flexible financing options.

Case Study: Building the Cheapest ADU Ever

Background:

Mary, a thrifty homeowner in Los Angeles, wanted to build the cheapest ADU possible in her backyard.

Her goal was to create a functional living space without breaking the bank.

Planning and Design:

Mary decided on a simple 400-square-foot detached ADU. She focused on essential features only, avoiding high-end finishes and complex designs.

She utilized online resources and DIY guides to create a cost-effective design plan.

Financing:

Mary had limited home equity and didn't want to take on a significant loan. She decided to finance her ADU through a combination of savings, a small personal loan, and sweat equity.

Construction:

Materials: Mary sourced reclaimed and second-hand materials from local salvage yards and online marketplaces. She purchased surplus building supplies at discounted prices.

Labor: To save on labor costs, Mary enlisted the help of friends and family for the construction work. She also did much of the work herself, including painting and installing fixtures.

Permits: She navigated the permitting process herself, carefully following local guidelines to avoid costly mistakes and delays.

Outcome:

The ADU was completed in six months, with a total cost of $25,000. Mary successfully created a functional and comfortable living space on a tight budget. She decided to rent it out to a college student, generating additional income.

Benefits Experienced:

Cost Savings: By using reclaimed materials and DIY labor, Mary significantly reduced construction costs.

Additional Income: Renting out the ADU provided a steady income stream.

Increased Property Value: The ADU added value to her property without a large financial investment.

Lessons Learned:

Resourcefulness: Sourcing second-hand materials and doing much of the work herself helped Mary keep costs low.

Community Support: Enlisting help from friends and family made the project feasible on a tight budget.

Thorough Planning: Careful planning and adherence to local regulations prevented costly mistakes and delays.

Conclusion

Financing an ADU project requires careful consideration of various options to find the best fit for your financial situation and project goals. Home equity loans, HELOCs, construction loans, government grants, and private financing each offer unique benefits and challenges.

By exploring these options and learning from real-life examples like Mary's, homeowners can make informed decisions and successfully finance their ADU projects.

Chapter 11: Common Challenges and How to Overcome Them

Building an Accessory Dwelling Unit (ADU) can be a rewarding project, but it comes with its own set of challenges. Understanding these potential obstacles and how to navigate them can help ensure a smoother process.

This chapter discusses common challenges in the ADU process, including permit navigation, cost management, construction delays, and tenant management, and provides practical advice on how to overcome them.

1. Permit Navigation

Challenges:

Complex Regulations: ADU projects must comply with a myriad of local, state, and sometimes federal regulations, which can be overwhelming.

Lengthy Approval Process: The approval process can be slow, with multiple stages of review and required modifications.

Solutions:

Research Local Regulations: Start by thoroughly researching your local zoning and building codes. Contact your city's planning department for guidance and use online resources to understand the specific requirements in your area.

Hire a Professional: Engage an architect or a permit expeditor who is familiar with the local permitting process. Their expertise can help navigate the complexities and expedite the approval process.

Prepare Thorough Documentation: Ensure all plans and documents are complete and accurate before submission.

Missing information can cause delays and additional scrutiny.

2. Cost Management

Challenges:

Budget Overruns: Construction projects often face budget overruns due to unforeseen issues, changes in material costs, or scope creep.

Financing Difficulties: Securing financing for an ADU can be challenging, especially for homeowners with limited equity or credit issues.

Solutions:

Detailed Budget Planning: Create a detailed budget that includes a contingency fund for unexpected expenses.

Track all expenditures carefully throughout the project.

Seek Multiple Bids: Obtain bids from several contractors to ensure you're getting a competitive price.

Review each bid thoroughly to understand what is included.

Explore Financing Options: Investigate various financing options early in the planning process.

Consider home equity loans, HELOCs, construction loans, and government grants. Choose the option that best fits your financial situation and project scope.

3. Construction Delays

Challenges:

Supply Chain Issues: Delays in obtaining materials can slow down the construction process.

Weather and Site Conditions: Adverse weather or unexpected site conditions can cause delays.

Solutions:

Build a Realistic Timeline: Develop a realistic project timeline that accounts for potential delays. Include buffer periods for key milestones.

Communicate Regularly with Contractors: Maintain regular communication with your contractor to stay updated on progress and address any issues promptly.

Plan for Flexibility: Be prepared to adjust your timeline and budget as needed.

Flexibility can help mitigate the impact of unforeseen delays.

4. Tenant Management

Challenges:

Finding Reliable Tenants: Securing reliable tenants who pay rent on time and maintain the property can be difficult.

Tenant Disputes: Managing disputes or issues with tenants can be stressful and time-consuming.

Solutions:

Screen Tenants Thoroughly: Conduct thorough background and credit checks on potential tenants. Contact previous landlords and verify employment to ensure reliability.

Clear Rental Agreements: Draft clear and comprehensive rental agreements that outline the responsibilities of both the landlord and tenant. Include clauses for maintenance, rent payment, and conflict resolution.

Property Management Services: Consider hiring a property management service if you prefer not to manage the rental process yourself.

These services can handle tenant screening, rent collection, and maintenance issues.

Case Study: Overcoming Challenges in an ADU Project

Background:

Mike and Lisa, homeowners in Encino, decided to build a detached ADU in their backyard to generate rental income. They faced several challenges, including permit navigation, budget management, construction delays, and tenant management.

Permit Navigation:

Mike and Lisa found the local permitting process complex and time-consuming. They hired an experienced architect who was familiar with Encino's ADU regulations.

The architect helped them prepare thorough documentation, which facilitated smoother approvals.

Cost Management:

To manage costs, they created a detailed budget with a contingency fund.

They obtained multiple bids from contractors and chose one that offered a competitive price and a detailed scope of work.

They also explored different financing options and secured a home equity line of credit (HELOC) to fund the project.

Construction Delays:

During construction, they faced delays due to supply chain issues.

To mitigate this, they maintained regular communication with their contractor and adjusted their timeline accordingly.

They also built flexibility into their schedule, which helped them manage the delays without significant stress.

Tenant Management:

After completing the ADU, Mike and Lisa wanted to ensure they found reliable tenants.

They conducted thorough screenings, including background checks and contacting previous landlords.

They also used a clear rental agreement that outlined all responsibilities and expectations.

To simplify tenant management, they decided to use a property management service, which handled rent collection and maintenance issues.

Outcome:

Despite the challenges, Mike and Lisa successfully completed their ADU project. They found reliable t

Tenants who paid rent on time and maintained the property well. The rental income significantly helped with their mortgage payments and increased their property's overall value.

Lessons Learned:

Professional Help: Hiring professionals for permit navigation and property management can save time and reduce stress.

Detailed Planning: Thorough planning and budget management are crucial for handling unexpected expenses and delays.

Flexibility: Building flexibility into your timeline and budget helps manage unforeseen challenges effectively.

Conclusion

Building an ADU comes with various challenges, but with careful planning and the right strategies, these obstacles can be overcome.

By understanding the potential issues in permit navigation, cost management, construction delays, and tenant management, homeowners can take proactive steps to ensure a successful ADU project.

Learning from real-life experiences, like those of Mike and Lisa, highlights the importance of professional guidance, thorough planning, and flexibility in achieving your ADU goals.

The Bright Future of Building an ADU

Building an Accessory Dwelling Unit (ADU) is a fantastic opportunity to enhance your property, generate additional income, and contribute to solving housing shortages.

As regulations become more supportive and streamlined, the process of adding an ADU has never been more accessible. By investing in an ADU, you are not only creating a valuable asset for your family but also promoting sustainable and efficient land use.

Imagine a future where your ADU provides a cozy home for a loved one, a flexible space for guests, or a steady source of rental income.

The potential benefits are vast, ranging from increased property value to the joy of creating a welcoming, independent living space.

With thoughtful planning and the right resources, you can transform your vision into reality, knowing you are making a positive impact on your community.

Embrace the journey of building your ADU with optimism and confidence. This endeavor not only enhances your lifestyle but also represents a step towards more sustainable and innovative housing solutions.

The future is bright, and your ADU is a cornerstone of that promising horizon.

Laws and Regulations in Los Angeles County and City

Key Differences Between Los Angeles City (LA City) and Los Angeles County (LA County)

Jurisdiction and Governance

Los Angeles City (LA City):

- **Governance:** Governed by the Los Angeles City Council and the Mayor of Los Angeles.

- **Jurisdiction:** Covers the specific geographic area within the city limits of Los Angeles.

- **Services:** Provides municipal services such as police, fire, public works, and zoning regulations specific to the city.

- **Regulations:** Has its own set of building codes, zoning laws, and municipal regulations that apply only within the city limits.

Los Angeles County (LA County):

- **Governance:** Governed by the Los Angeles County Board of Supervisors.

- **Jurisdiction:** Encompasses a much larger area that includes 88 incorporated cities (including LA City) and many unincorporated areas.

- **Services:** Provides regional services such as health services, social services, public transportation, and sheriff's department coverage for unincorporated areas.

Also provides services to smaller cities within the county that do not have their own municipal services.

- **Regulations:** Has county-wide regulations that apply to unincorporated areas and sometimes provide additional regulations that cities within the county may adopt.

Size and Scope:

LA City: A single city with a population of approximately 4 million people, covering about 503 square miles.

LA County: A vast county with a population of over 10 million people, covering about 4,751 square miles, including numerous cities and unincorporated areas.

Services:

LA City: Focuses on services for residents within the city limits, including LAPD and LAFD.

LA County: Provides broader regional services, including the LA County Sheriff's Department and LA County Fire Department, especially for unincorporated areas.

Public Services and Infrastructure:

LA City: Manages its own public infrastructure, such as roads, parks, and libraries within the city.

LA County: Manages county-wide infrastructure projects and services that benefit multiple cities and unincorporated areas.

ADU Regulations

Los Angeles County:

Permitted Zones: ADUs are allowed in most residential zones, subject to specific requirements for setbacks, height limits, and parking.

Regulatory Compliance: ADUs must comply with both local development standards and state law requirements under Government Code Sections 65852.2.

Permit Requirements: Obtaining permits involves zoning review, building permits, and inspections to ensure compliance with all regulations.

City of Los Angeles:

Streamlined Processes: Recent state laws (e.g., AB 68, AB 881, SB 13) have streamlined the ADU approval process, reducing permit approval times and limiting local restrictions.

Zoning and Permits:

- Residential Lots: ADUs are allowed on most residentially zoned lots.

- Multi-Family Properties: Multiple ADUs may be allowed on multi-family properties.

- Parking Requirements: No additional parking is required if the property is within ½ mile of public transit.

Size and Regulations:

- Maximum Size: Detached ADUs can be up to 1,200 square feet.
- Movable Tiny Houses: Specific guidelines apply, requiring DMV registration and ANSI or NFPA compliance certification.

Practical Implications for Homeowners

Permits and Regulations:

LA City: If you're building an ADU or making significant changes to your property, you need to follow the city's specific permitting process and regulations.

LA County: If your property is in an unincorporated area of the county, you will follow the county's regulations and permitting process. If your property is within an incorporated city other than LA City, you will follow that city's regulations, which may be influenced by county policies.

Services:

LA City: Services like trash collection, street maintenance, and local policing are managed by the city.

LA County: These services might be managed by the county for unincorporated areas or provided by local municipalities in incorporated cities.

Understanding these differences is crucial for homeowners, especially when dealing with property modifications, construction, or utilizing public services.

Useful Resources:

These resources provide detailed information about ADU types, benefits, and regulations specific to Los Angeles County and City, helping homeowners and renters navigate the process and make informed decisions.

LA County Planning ADUs

LA City ADU Guidelines

GreatBuildz Los Angeles ADU Guide

California Department of Housing and Community Development

Los Angeles Department of Building and Safety

Made in United States
Troutdale, OR
10/16/2024

23792920R00042